NOBODY MOVE
(JOURNAL FOR MEMORIES)

ROBERT ESPOSITO

Nobody Move! (Journal For Memories)

Copyright © 2024 by *Robert Esposito*

All rights reserved.

Published by Red Penguin Books

Library of Congress Control Number: 2025927751

ISBN: 978-1-63777-738-1

No part of this book may be reproduced in any form or by any electronic or mechanical means, including information storage and retrieval systems, without written permission from the author, except for the use of brief quotations in a book review.

TABLE OF CONTENTS

AUTHOR'S NOTE 1

THE PAST: LOOKING BACK AND TAKING INVENTORY 5

THE PRESENT: THE MOVE AND TRANSITIONING 21

THE FUTURE: HOPES FOR THE NEW HOUSE 27

CONCLUDE BY CLEANING OUT THE CLOSET 35

ABOUT THE AUTHOR 45

"Remember you didn't just move your things; whether it be for better or for worse; you moved your life forward. This transition is part of your journey."

—Robert Esposito

AUTHOR'S NOTE

The below few paragraphs I placed in the very beginning of Nobody Move (Without Reading This.) Here I describe the four main circumstances in which someone moves throughout their life. In order to familiarize yourself with the four circumstances here they are.

The poem, "Reason, Season and a Lifetime" by Brian A. "Drew" Chalker is about the way people come in and out of your life. People always have to move in life, whether for a reason or a season, and sometimes, it's for a lifetime. When you figure out which it is, you'll know better what to do.

The majority, if not all, of the moves that take place in your life will happen under one of the four circumstances below:

The first instance is when your caretaker is making you move because, well, they are your caretaker and they are moving. This move can be simple, like a family moving across town. You often hear people say, "I want to move now before the kids get settled in school."

Next as you become a young adult is through achievements and moving through life's stages. You may be going to college, moving for a new job or promotion, moving to the city or the suburbs, getting married, getting a bigger house or downsizing, or retiring.

A little further on can also be through nonachievements in life's stages. (I want to pause to say I chose "nonachievements" instead of "failures" intentionally. What we consider failures differs with each person and is usually based on perception.) These nonachievements could be divorce, loss of job, career change, family reasons, damage, natural disaster, etc.

Then, finally, it goes full circle and the people you cared for now care for you. Maybe you're children of adult parents who are moving mom and dad close to home to make sure they have the help they need. Or, maybe you're moving an adult parent into an assisted living facility, a nursing home, to a healthier climate, or perhaps shipping them out on ice floes when they can no longer contribute.

So, as you can see we have major and minor life events that cause us to move. We also have positive, non positive, and perhaps negative, reasons for moving. I suggest no matter the reason, or the season of your life, you should still utilize this journal. Some people enjoy journaling. Personally, I never kept one for that long of a time period. However, I did journal randomly throughout my life, usually for a year or so at a time. It is always so intriguing when I stumble upon one of my old note pads or journals. I bring myself back to that time and that mind set and relish in the trip down memory lane.

I've talked a lot about the stress of moving. I make it a point to drill down that the stress is not just the logistical stress of moving day. The stress is the emotional stress of all that comes before and after moving. As well as in some instances the event or events that set in motion the reason for actually moving. Moving is the personification of the transition of a chapter of your life. A physical event that transfers you from one place to another, one part of your journey to the next.

Whether or not you usually keep a journal, I encourage you to use the outline below to jot down a few memories from this time in your life. You don't have to answer every question—just pick the ones that speak to you most.

After all, this transition is a chapter in your story that will never happen again. You may be grateful to have these memories written down someday.

THE GHOSTS OF PAST, PRESENT, AND FUTURE!

THE PAST: LOOKING BACK AND TAKING INVENTORY

"The first time the world has you crazy; and you yearn towards your house for solace; it is at this moment when your house becomes your home."

— Robert Esposito

THE PAST: LOOKING BACK AND TAKING INVENTORY

What brought you to the location you are leaving?

What were your goals as you were moving in?

Did you achieve them?

_____

What were your failures during this timeframe?

_____

THE PAST: LOOKING BACK AND TAKING INVENTORY

Are you able to see value in those failures and define them as lessons that you needed for your journey?

_____
_____
_____
_____
_____
_____
_____
_____
_____
_____
_____

What advice would you give yourself if you could go back to move-in day?

_____
_____
_____
_____
_____
_____
_____
_____
_____
_____
_____

Describe the day in this house you felt the most warmth, the most love?

_____
_____
_____
_____
_____
_____
_____
_____
_____

Describe the night in this home when you felt the coldest, loneliest, or most unsettled. What happened and how did you cope?

_____
_____
_____
_____
_____
_____
_____
_____
_____

What kind of purpose and/or lessons did you take away from each of these nights?

What did this house teach you about resilience, patience, or love?

What was one holiday or celebration that defined this house for you?

THE PAST: LOOKING BACK AND TAKING INVENTORY

What traditions did you start in this house?

_____
_____
_____
_____
_____
_____
_____
_____
_____
_____
_____
_____

What was your favorite small detail about this house?

_____
_____
_____
_____
_____
_____
_____
_____
_____
_____
_____
_____

What piece of furniture or object holds the most memories from this house?

Where was your favorite spot to sit and think, cry, or dream? Why?

If the walls could talk, what unforgettable moment would they share?

What would you thank this home for, if you could?

Did any part of this home ever frustrate you to the point of making you laugh? Describe it.

_____
_____
_____
_____
_____
_____
_____
_____
_____
_____

What could never be fixed on this house no matter what you did?

_____
_____
_____
_____
_____
_____
_____
_____
_____
_____

What will you not miss about this old house?

What was the hardest goodbye you had to make in this house?

If this house could write YOU a goodbye letter, what would it say?

_____
_____
_____
_____
_____
_____
_____
_____
_____
_____

Was there a "hidden gem" in your old neighborhood you'll miss?

_____
_____
_____
_____
_____
_____
_____
_____
_____
_____

How did your community make your time here special?

What are three things you wish you could tell the next person who will live here?

THE PRESENT: THE MOVE AND TRANSITIONING

"No doubt the universe is unfolding as it should. Therefore be at peace with God, whatever you conceive Him to be. And whatever your labors and aspirations, in the noisy confusion of life, keep peace in your soul. With all its sham, drudgery and broken dreams, it is still a beautiful world. Be cheerful. Strive to be happy."

– Max Ehrmann

22

THE PRESENT: THE MOVE AND TRANSITIONING

What set in motion the change in your life to move on from this location?

What do you want to say or remember about this chapter of your journey?

What surprised you most as you packed and prepared to leave?

Did Nobody Move (WITHOUT READING THIS) help make this new transition the easiest logistical one on record?

THE PRESENT: THE MOVE AND TRANSITIONING

What is one item you're packing that holds the most meaning, and why?

What emotions surprised you most during this move?

What moment during this move made you proud of yourself?

THE FUTURE: HOPES FOR THE NEW HOUSE

3

"For better or worse, no matter what, and despite your feelings; this transition is just another new beginning on your journey!"

— Robert Esposito

28

THE FUTURE: HOPES FOR THE NEW HOUSE

What is your strongest feeling about your new chapter?

What are some of your goals for this next chapter of your life?

What are some of your fears for this next chapter of your life?

_____
_____
_____
_____
_____
_____
_____
_____
_____
_____

What new traditions would you like to carry on from your old home and what new ones would you like to create here?

_____
_____
_____
_____
_____
_____
_____
_____
_____
_____
_____
_____

THE FUTURE: HOPES FOR THE NEW HOUSE

What "New Year's resolution" type changes do you commit to making during this next chapter?

What lesson about "home" will you take with you into your next chapter?

What are you most looking forward to discovering in your new home or neighborhood?

THE FUTURE: HOPES FOR THE NEW HOUSE

Describe a scene you would like to see in this new house five years from now.

CONCLUDE BY CLEANING OUT THE CLOSET

"Mental health is not a destination, but a process. It's about how you drive, not where you're going."

– Noam Shpancer, PHD.

36

CONCLUDE BY CLEANING OUT THE CLOSET

This is YOUR conclusion. This is not my conclusion. This is for you and your family and anyone you let read it. Be it a time to reminisce, a time to remember something you are having trouble thinking of, or just a time to reflect; this section is yours to do as you please.

I remember some time ago I saw an episode of Freakonomics on the History Channel. It was about a book on how to be a good parent for expecting adults. The narrator explained how you do not need to read the book; just by simply being the type of person to buy the book makes you a better parent-to-be than someone who does not care to buy the book in hopes of preparing.

Be proud of yourself; because the simple act of you reading this means you care, value yourself, your family, and are willing to do the work to better yourself.

My Reflections

Use this space to capture additional memories, thoughts, lessons, or emotions from your moving journey.

Goodbye Letter to My Old Home

Write a personal farewell message to the home you are leaving behind.

Gratitude List

List the things you are most grateful for from your time in your old home and community.

CONCLUDE BY CLEANING OUT THE CLOSET

Vision for My New Home

Dream about how you want your new home to feel, look, and support your life journey.

Write a farewell message to the old chapter of your life:

CONCLUDE BY CLEANING OUT THE CLOSET

" I wish you peace on your journey into your new beginning. I urge you to ask family members questions from above when you deem suited. You are free to write as you please, for this is my—The End."

Robert Esposito

ABOUT THE AUTHOR

Robert Esposito

Published Author, Entrepreneur, and Founder of Relocators

Robert Esposito is the founder of Relocators, a multi-dimensional end-to-end home transition company. Esposito started the company in 2008, but the seed was planted years prior. In early 2000, his Nana was diagnosed with breast cancer and his mother was tasked with clearing out her home in Queens, New York and moving her to Long Island. After this emotionally and physically difficult move, his mom started Sisters In Charge, which was one of Long Island's first estate sale companies.

Esposito was tasked with helping his mother's clients clean out their homes after the estate sales. As a young entrepreneur, he saw how the industry was fragmented and in 2008, borrowed $4000 from his family to purchase his first used box truck and Relocators Service Inc. was born.

Today, Esposito has grown what was once a small family business started by his mother into a highly-respected regional moving company with six locations in New York and Florida. Relocators specializes in local and long distance residential moving, home clean-out and junk removal, professional estate sales, online auctions, and secure storage. They are also a top vendor handling restoration pack-outs by assisting restoration companies, major insurance carriers, and adjusters.

Esposito understands that moving is one of life's biggest stressors and with over 20 years of experience, has built a company that takes the stress, worry, and concern out of moving by providing a seamless, end-to-end solution. He is involved in every aspect of the daily operations and takes pride in helping families easily transition to their next chapter. As a leader, he's built a team that shares that same commitment. Every staff member is trained to offer personal guidance, so each customer feels supported and cared for through every step of the process.

A personal branding and networking expert, Esposito regularly appears on podcasts and speaks to business groups, educating his audience about entrepreneurship and how to lead and grow a business.

Epsosito received his bachelor's degree in human relations with a minor in theology and acting from St. Joseph's College in Patchogue, New York.

His first book, Nobody Move (Without Reading This), recently landed a five-book publishing deal with Stephanie Larkin of Red Penguin Publishing. The book also won an International Book Award in the category of Real Estate. The book is packed with practical tips and real-life stories to help anyone facing a move feel less overwhelmed. Designed to be more than just a guide for individuals—it's a powerful tool for professionals, as well. Real estate agents, mortgage brokers, and anyone guiding clients through big transitions can use it as a thoughtful gift or a go-to resource, giving

ABOUT THE AUTHOR

their clients something tangible to lean on during one of life's most stressful moments.

Nobodymovebook.com

"*I wish for you closure if you're navigating an ending, excitement if an achievement has been met, and most importantly, happiness either way as you approach your new beginning.*"

—Robert Esposito
Nobody Move (Without Reading This)
Chapter: The Author's Note
Page: 2